THINK BIGGER

THE
REAL MAN
HANDBOOK

by
Michael Berg

PREFACE
THE LEGACY OF A REAL MAN

I stood in silence at my grandfather's grave—his final resting place beside the woman he loved. The Sacramento Valley National Cemetery holds the remains of many heroes, but I knew his story ran deeper than what was etched in stone. A lieutenant colonel in the United States Air Force, he flew in World War II, Korea, and Vietnam. But his real strength wasn't just in the skies—it was in how he lived: with purpose, with dignity, and with quiet power.

At his funeral, I shook the hands of veterans well into their nineties. Their grips were steady. Their eyes were clear. There was something unmistakable about them—an unshakable confidence, discipline, and sense of mission. These were men of another era. They were Real Men.

Later, I knelt alone before my grandparents' grave and prayed—for guidance, for clarity, for strength to become the kind of man he had been. As I drove away, a single question weighed on my heart:

Where have all the real men gone?

Today, masculinity is being misunderstood, mocked, and reshaped into something unrecognizable. Young men are pressured to deny their instincts, question their wiring, and suppress what makes them male. In a world that once honored the natural differences between men and women—what was once common sense now feels controversial.

We've gone from Men are from Mars, Women are from Venus to a generation that's not even sure which planet they're supposed to be on. Masculinity isn't just misunderstood—it's being erased, rewritten, and replaced with noise. Personal pronouns have become louder than personal responsibility. And boys are growing up with more labels than they are role models.

This is for the son learning what it means to lead. This is for the husband learning to love with strength. This is for the man who knows there's more inside of him.

Real manhood doesn't need redefinition. It needs restoration.

This book is not just a guide. It's a challenge. A call to rise. A blueprint for reclaiming what it means to be a man in a world that desperately needs men of strength, vision, and integrity.

Let this book help you unlock that man.

PROLOGUE

THINK BIGGER

The world is growing louder—but weaker. We're surrounded by opinions, distractions, and identities, but we're starving for truth. For strength. For direction.

What we need now isn't more voices shouting into the void. We need more **Real Men**—men with backbone, vision, and conviction.

Men who know who they are and live it boldly. Men who build more than brands—they build families, futures, and foundations. Men who don't just show up—they lead, protect, and leave a mark.

Being a man of character isn't about dominating others; it's about mastering yourself. It's not about looking tough; it's about being tough when it counts. It's not about old-school machismo; it's about modern mastery of oneself.

This book isn't here to flatter you. It's here to **challenge** you.

Because somewhere along the way, masculinity got lost. Not because it stopped mattering—but because we stopped fighting for it.

We now live in a culture where boys are told to be ashamed of their strength, unsure of their roles, and confused about what manhood even is. We've raised a generation who don't know whether to step up or stand down—because no one ever showed them how.

This isn't evolution—it's the aftermath.

The world doesn't just need men who feel—it needs men who act. Men who move with discipline. Men who own their responsibilities and don't flinch when it's hard. Men who don't chase affirmation—they build identity through effort.

This book is a call to come back to what never should've been lost: Faith. Leadership. Character. Discipline. Respect. Brotherhood. Purpose. Courage.

You'll be challenged to look inward, stand taller, and live louder—not with ego, but with excellence. Each chapter ends with a clear Challenge because talk is cheap, and real men take action.

If you've ever felt like you were made for more, it's because you were.

This is more than a handbook.
It's a reset. A standard. A call to rise.

The world is watching—and waiting—for men to be men again. Let's show them how. Let's rebuild the foundation. Let's reclaim masculinity. **Let's think bigger.**

CHAPTER ONE

FAITH:
THE COMPASS OF A REAL MAN

Faith is more than religion. It is the invisible force that strengthens a man when his strength is gone. It is the unshakable belief that there is something greater than himself—something bigger than his pain, his struggle, his ego, and even his own ambition. In a time when self-reliance is glorified, faith reminds us we were never meant to carry the weight of life alone.

You don't need to subscribe to one specific religion to understand faith. Every culture and tradition across the globe hold a concept of it. These traditions, including Islam, Christianity, and Judaism, once coexisted in peace—sharing a rich history of philosophy, worship, and community. Though conflict has marked certain eras, history has also shown that these faiths can live in harmony, united by shared moral values and reverence for the divine:

Islam sees faith (Iman) as both a deep personal belief and a visible commitment through action—prayer, charity, and fasting are its daily rhythms. Christianity teaches that faith is the substance of things hoped for, the evidence of things not seen, empowering believers to walk by trust, not sight. Judaism integrates faith with action; belief is expressed through deeds, tradition, and community responsibility. Hinduism encourages connection to the divine within through faith, service, and devotion. Buddhism grounds faith in self-awareness, practice, and inner transformation. Stoicism, while not theistic, finds spiritual ground in accepting the natural order and cultivating inner virtue.

Faith is universal because the need for meaning is worldwide. Men crave purpose. Without it, we drift. We chase distractions. We numb dissatisfaction. But with belief, we become anchored— men on mission.

Embracing belief isn't weakness; it's wisdom. It takes humility to recognize limitations and strength to release control. Faith builds from the inside out.

Belief disciplines the mind and calms the heart. It doesn't act on impulse but on grounded values. It brings clarity to speech and intention to choices. Faith reveals that life is more than tasks—it's a sacred assignment.

One young man, uncertain of his future, went to live with monks in Nepal. He wasn't religious—he was seeking peace. In their silence and routine, he discovered that faith wasn't about rules; it was about devotion. Every action, from sweeping the floor to sharing a meal, was done with care. He returned home with a renewed mission to serve his community with the same purpose and humility. That was faith in motion.

Another story: a soldier caught in an ambush. He later said it wasn't courage that saved him—it was an inner voice that said, "Stay calm. You're not alone." Though he'd never prayed before, he survived and committed his life to mentoring others. Faith found him in the fire—and it transformed him.

This is where the foundation of influence is laid.

Faith shapes influence not by force, but by example. It's the quiet consistency of a man who honors his word, even when it costs him. It's the strength behind kindness, the steadiness behind truth, and the courage behind conviction.

A man of faith doesn't need a spotlight to make an impact. His presence speaks louder than his position. He influences not by controlling others, but by embodying what he believes. His life becomes a message—one that says integrity still matters, compassion still heals, and character still counts.

It's the father who tucks his kids in with a prayer, even after a long day. The friend who shows up when things fall apart, not with answers, but with presence. The stranger who helps without expecting anything in return, simply because it's right.

Influence through faith is subtle but profound. It changes atmospheres. It calms storms. It inspires courage in others—not by commanding it, but by carrying it. It reminds those around us that hope is not naïve, and goodness is not weakness.

History is full of those whose influence was rooted in faith. Men who changed the world not by overpowering it, but by standing firmly in what they believed. Their legacy wasn't built in moments of glory—but in the decisions they made when no one was watching.

That is the essence of influence through faith: quiet, steady, unshakable. Not loud, but lasting. Not flashy, but foundational.

And when storms come—and they will—it's faith that anchors influence, reminding us that what we stand for speaks far louder than what we say.

Before Chick-fil-A became a household name, Samuel Truett Cathy was just a man with a Bible, a grill, and an unwavering conviction. Born in 1921 in Eatonton, Georgia, Cathy grew up in poverty during the Great Depression. While others bent to survive, Truett stood on a rock-solid faith that would shape every decision he made—even when it cost him.

Cathy opened his first restaurant, the Dwarf Grill, in 1946. From the start, he made an uncommon choice: closing on Sundays. It wasn't about business—it was about honoring God, resting, and keeping priorities straight. That one principle would become a cornerstone of Chick-fil-A, even as competitors warned it would kill profits. It didn't. In fact, it made the brand stand out.

But Cathy's faith wasn't a Sunday-only affair. He personally taught Sunday school to teenage boys for over 50 years. He invested in foster homes, scholarships, and youth mentoring—not for publicity, but because he believed it was a man's duty to build the next generation. He once said, "We must motivate ourselves to do our very best, and by our example lead others to do their best as well."

Even when Chick-fil-A exploded into a billion-dollar empire, Cathy never compromised. He refused to go public with stock to keep control of the company's values. He turned down offers that would've made him richer, all to preserve what he felt God had entrusted to him.

Cathy's story isn't about chicken. It's about conviction. He modeled what it means to be a real man—faithful, disciplined, generous, and guided by something bigger than profit.

Faith anchors a man in divine purpose, elevates his vision above the noise, and ignites the courage to lead, the resilience to endure, and the wisdom to leave a mark that lasts.

Faith is the fire that burns quietly within. Tend to it daily and let it guide you.

Once a man anchors his life in something greater than himself, the next step is clear: he must lead. Not for applause—but because his faith compels him to act.

TAKE ACTION ON THESE THREE CHALLENGES.

1. Reflect: What do you believe in beyond yourself? Write it down.
2. Practice: Spend 10 minutes daily in prayer, silence, or sacred reading. Ask, *Am I aligned with what I say I believe?*
3. Act: Live one day this week as if your beliefs were the foundation of every decision. Notice the difference.

CHAPTER TWO

LEADERSHIP:
OWNING THE WEIGHT OF INFLUENCE

Leadership doesn't begin when a man is handed a position—it begins when he accepts responsibility. It shows up in how he carries himself, how he treats others, and how he navigates life's hardest moments. True leadership starts within.

Before anyone follows you, they watch you. They observe your patterns. They notice your posture in conflict, your patience under pressure, and your principles when no one's looking. Leadership is built in silence—long before it's ever recognized out loud.

Think back to the men who shaped your life. Maybe it was a father or uncle who always showed up, even after a long day. Maybe it was a teacher who believed in you when you doubted yourself. Or a boss who didn't just give orders, but taught you how to think, how to grow, how to rise. Those moments were leadership in motion—not flashy, not loud—but deeply felt.

Every man is born with the capacity to lead. But not every man chooses to develop that capacity. Leadership isn't natural. It's cultivated. It's sharpened through adversity, challenge, and the daily grind of life. It's not found in charisma. It's found in character.

And it starts with self-leadership.

You can't lead others if you haven't learned to lead yourself—your thoughts, your habits, your time, your emotions. Without internal discipline, external leadership becomes hollow. That's why before we talk about faith and how it connects to leadership, we must first understand the weight of influence that already rests on our shoulders.

Every man leads—even if he doesn't realize it. He leads with his presence or his absence. With his silence or his voice. With his example or his excuses. The question isn't whether he influences people—it's how.

Leadership isn't about being in charge. It's about being accountable. It's about walking into a room and making people feel safer, clearer, more focused—not because you have all the answers, but because you're anchored in who you are.

Before faith gives a man the compass, before leadership becomes service—there must be a decision: to own that influence. To stop outsourcing blame. To stop shrinking back. To stop waiting for someone else to step up.

That's where leadership begins.

Leadership isn't a title. It's a daily decision. It's the weight a man carries when others look to him—not for answers alone, but for steadiness, direction, and trust. Influence doesn't always come with a microphone or spotlight. Often, it comes quietly through consistency, presence, and unwavering principles.

At its core, leadership is service. It's the art of lifting others while remaining grounded. A true leader doesn't command attention—he earns respect. He listens more than he speaks, and when he does speak, his words carry weight because they are backed by action.

Think of a man building a home. Not just walls and a roof, but a safe place—one brick, one nail, one beam at a time. That's how leadership is forged. Not in grand gestures, but in the unseen moments: following through on commitments, speaking truth when it's hard, encouraging growth, and showing up—especially when it's inconvenient.

Consider a story from South Africa. A community plagued by violence and hopelessness found peace not through politics, but through a quiet elder. Every morning, he swept the village square. He greeted neighbors by name. When disputes broke out, he'd invite both parties to sit with him under a tree. He asked questions. He listened. His wisdom wasn't loud, but it shaped generations. That's leadership.

Or think of a single father raising three kids, working nights, cooking dinner, and helping with homework. He doesn't complain. He shows up. Not because it's easy, but because his role is vital. That's leadership.

Leadership doesn't mean having all the answers. It means creating space where others can grow into their best selves. It's choosing integrity over popularity, responsibility over comfort, and courage over complacency.

Faith and leadership go hand-in-hand. One grounds the man, the other guides his steps. Together, they shape how he influences his family, his workplace, his community, and even himself.

Whether in sacred texts or modern history, the best leaders practiced humility and vision. Gandhi led barefoot, not to be praised, but to embody simplicity. Marcus Aurelius ruled an empire, yet kept journals reminding himself to remain just and calm. Prophet Muhammad lived among his people—eating with them, praying beside them, carrying wood for fires.

Leadership is never about self-promotion. It's about self-mastery.

What makes a man worth following isn't perfection. It's perseverance. It's his ability to stand firm in storms, admit his mistakes, and rise stronger. It's choosing to do right even when no one applauds.

Every man has influence—whether he realizes it or not. People are watching. A younger brother. A coworker. A son. A neighbor. A friend. The question isn't whether he leads. The question is: ***How?***

Colin Powell, the first African American U.S. Secretary of State and a four-star general, was a model of servant leadership in action. Born in Harlem to Jamaican immigrants, Powell rose through the ranks not because of ego—but because of discipline, competence, and integrity.

As a young soldier, he was known for working harder than anyone else and for leading by example, not position. He famously said, *"Leadership is solving problems. The day soldiers stop bringing you their problems is the day you have stopped leading them."* His leadership wasn't about dominating a room—it was about taking responsibility when things went wrong and giving credit when things went right.

Powell believed in the power of clear values and decision-making under pressure. He once shared his "13 Rules of Leadership," which included things like *"It can be done,"* and *"Avoid having your ego so close to your position that when your position falls, your ego goes with it."*

His calm under fire, his ability to connect across political divides, and his clear sense of duty made him a true example of how real leadership is forged—not through charisma alone, but through competence, consistency, and character.

The world doesn't need louder men. It needs steadier ones. Men who can carry the weight. Who protect, provide, and guide—not for recognition, but because it's right.

That's what leadership looks like.

You are already a leader. The only question is what kind.

Leadership may open the door, but character is what keeps you in the room. Without it, your influence is hollow. That's where we go next.

TAKE ACTION ON THESE THREE CHALLENGES.

1. Reflect: Where in your life are you already leading? Where are you needed most?
2. Practice: Choose one person this week to encourage, support, or guide—without being asked.
3. Evaluate: Do your daily actions align with the kind of leader you want to be? If not, make one change starting now.

CHAPTER THREE

CHARACTER:
THE FOUNDATION THAT LASTS

You can impress people with talent. You can gain attention with looks, money, or charm. But character? Character is what remains when everything else fades. It's the core of who you are—the invisible structure that holds your life together.

Character is not built in comfort. It's forged in resistance. Formed in silence. Revealed in pressure. A man's true measure isn't seen when he's on stage—it's shown in how he acts when no one is watching, when the stakes are high, and when doing the right thing costs him something.

In today's world, it's easy to prioritize appearance over integrity. Social media teaches men to perform rather than to persevere. But image without substance collapses. What lasts is deeper. Character is what people remember long after the applause fades.

Character begins long before adulthood. It starts in the early lessons that shape how a boy sees himself and others. It's formed when he chooses not to lie about breaking the vase. When he helps a friend instead of laughing with the crowd. When he owns up to a mistake, even if it means facing consequences. These moments, small and unnoticed, are the seeds of character.

As boys grow into men, the tests change—but the principle remains: Will you do what's right, even when it's hard?

In today's culture, those choices are harder than ever. A college freshman once shared how he created a second Instagram account just to show off a lifestyle he didn't really live—renting expensive clothes, taking staged photos in borrowed cars. He felt pressure to match the image of success his peers projected. But behind the screen, he was anxious, isolated, and unsure of who he really was. Eventually, he deleted the account and started over. Not with filters—but with truth. He said, 'For the first time, I felt free.' Social media has become a stage where people curate highlight reels and craft images instead of identities. The pressure to be liked, to look successful, to prove something—it's relentless. And for many young men, the temptation is strong: create the illusion instead of living the truth.

But character isn't curated. It's consistent. It's not about the brand you project—it's about the man you become.

Every time you post, speak, choose, or react—you're shaping your character. Not the one online. The one in real life. And while image fades, character stays. It's what people trust. It's what they feel in your presence, long before they see your résumé.

The earlier character is nurtured, the stronger it becomes. Parents, mentors, coaches, and communities have a role to play—but so does every young man. Even in a world of filters and fast likes, there's still power in being genuine. In standing for something. In doing what's right—not for the likes, but for the legacy.

It starts with honesty.

Tell the truth. Even when it's hard. Even when it's uncomfortable. Even when you stand alone. Truth is the bedrock of trust, and without trust, no relationship—personal or professional—can thrive. A man of character values his word. When he says he'll do something, he does it. Not to impress—but because it's who he is.

Character shows up in consistency. In how you treat people who can't benefit you. In how you handle anger, failure, and rejection. It's easy to act honorable when life is smooth. The test is how you act when you're under fire.

There's a story of a small-town mechanic who worked for forty years without fanfare. He was never late. He fixed every car like it belonged to his own mother. When asked why he never cut corners, he said, "Because that car carries someone's daughter. Someone's son. Their life matters."

That's character.

Another man, a high-powered executive, was offered a bribe to secure a deal that would've made him millions. No one would've known. But he walked away. Why? Because his integrity was worth more than any paycheck. That decision cost him short-term gains—but it gained him long-term trust and respect.

He remembered sitting across from his grandfather, who once said, "A man's word is his bond—never break it." Years later, that same truth echoed in a conversation with an imam who spoke of *amanah*, the sacred duty of being trustworthy. A pastor he met during a service reminded him, "The fruit of real faith is how you treat people—patience, self-control, humility."

Those lessons stuck. Different paths, same core: true strength is character.

Faith gives a man vision. Leadership gives him influence. But character—character is what gives him credibility.

Character is your legacy. Not what you owned, but what you stood for. Not how loud you were, but how deeply you lived.

It's what your children will say about you. It's what your coworkers will remember. It's what echoes when your voice is no longer here.

Pat Tillman was a starting safety in the NFL, playing for the Arizona Cardinals. He had everything a young man could want— fame, money, and a rising career. But after the attacks on 9/11, Tillman made a decision that shocked the sports world: he walked away from a multi-million-dollar contract to enlist in the U.S. Army.

He wasn't seeking headlines. He didn't make a public show of it. He simply believed it was the right thing to do. He served as an Army Ranger, completing multiple tours in combat zones. Tragically, Pat Tillman was killed in Afghanistan by friendly fire—an incident that became public controversy. But throughout the confusion and headlines, what never came into question was this: Pat Tillman lived with integrity.

He believed in personal responsibility. He followed his convictions, not the crowd. He once said, *"Somewhere inside, we hear a voice. It leads us in the direction of the person we wish to become."*

Tillman didn't just talk about values—he lived them. His story reminds us that character often means doing what's right even when no one's clapping. It means sacrificing comfort for conviction. He gave everything—not for recognition, but because he believed in something greater than himself.

Building character doesn't mean perfection. It means alignment. That your actions match your values. That your public life mirrors your private one. That your habits match your vision.

Character is the quiet force that shapes your world. Build it strong. Build it daily.

So how do you build character?

- Do the hard thing when no one is watching.
- Choose courage over comfort.
- Speak truth with love.
- Own your mistakes. Learn from them.
- Show up. Every day. Especially when you don't feel like it.

Because in the end, success without character is empty. But even quiet lives, lived with integrity, shake the world. Character is your compass—but without discipline, you drift. Character tells you what's right. Discipline is what helps you do it.

TAKE ACTION ON THESE THREE CHALLENGES.

1. Reflect: Where in your life is your character being tested right now?
2. Act: Do one thing today that aligns with your highest values—even if no one sees it.
3. Speak: Have one honest conversation this week you've been avoiding. Let truth lead.

CHAPTER FOUR

DISCIPLINE:
DOING WHAT MUST BE DONE

Every man wrestles with self-discipline. We all have areas where we fall short—habits we know we need to change, routines we mean to improve, goals we keep delaying. And yet, almost every man carries the quiet desire to do better. To wake up earlier. To waste less time. To take his health, his work, his purpose more seriously.

The intention is there—but the follow-through? That's where the struggle begins.

Discipline is the bridge between the man you are and the man you want to be. It's not about perfection—it's about progress. It's the ability to say no to what's easy, so you can say yes to what truly matters. It's showing up when it's inconvenient, following through when no one's watching, and staying the course when quitting would be simpler.

This is where most men get stuck—not because they're weak, but because life is loud. Responsibilities pile up. Distractions multiply. And slowly, self-discipline slips to the side.

But discipline doesn't need to be extreme. It needs to be consistent. It doesn't demand you become someone else—it invites you to become who you already are beneath the noise.

It's what transforms good intentions into real outcomes—and separates boys from men.

In a culture built on comfort and convenience, discipline is a disappearing virtue. We're told to follow our feelings, to rest when it's hard, to quit if it's not fun. But the path to greatness never runs through ease. It runs through endurance.

Discipline doesn't shout. It doesn't seek applause. It's quiet, steady, and often invisible to the world—but deeply felt in your results, your confidence, and your peace of mind.

A high school wrestler once shared his story. He wasn't the fastest or strongest on the team, but he made a decision: he would be the most consistent. While others skipped morning runs, he showed up. While teammates cheated reps in practice, he finished his sets. He won fewer matches early on, but by senior year, he became team captain and led them to a state championship. Not because he was naturally gifted—but because he was relentlessly disciplined.

Discipline begins with small choices: waking up on time, putting down the phone, finishing what you start. And it grows with each decision to keep going when excuses feel more comfortable than effort.

It sharpens your mind, strengthens your body, and shapes your will. Discipline isn't punishment. It's preparation.

A man without discipline is ruled by impulse. He reacts instead of responds. He drifts instead of decides. But when a man embraces discipline, he takes ownership of his time, his energy, his outcomes. He becomes dependable—not just to others, but to himself.

Faith provides the why. Character builds the integrity. Leadership carries the influence. But discipline? That's the engine that keeps it all moving.

Discipline has always been woven into the lives of men who made a lasting impact—not just through faith, but through focused, consistent effort over time. Consider Theodore Roosevelt, who overcame childhood asthma and physical weakness through sheer willpower, turning himself into a soldier, explorer, and president who lived with relentless energy.

Look at athletes like Michael Jordan, who is widely regarded as the greatest basketball player of all time. But what made him legendary wasn't just talent—it was a ferocious commitment to discipline. While most fans remember the dunks, game-winners, and championship rings, those closest to him saw the quiet grind long before the lights came on.

During his early days with the Chicago Bulls, Jordan wasn't just the most athletic guy on the floor—he was also the most obsessive. He arrived at the gym before anyone else, stayed after practice to shoot hundreds of free throws, and spent hours perfecting footwork drills others saw as boring or beneath them. To Jordan, discipline wasn't optional. It was the price of greatness.

Coach Phil Jackson recalled that Jordan would often ask to redo entire segments of practice if a single mistake disrupted the flow. "Repetition builds rhythm, and rhythm builds confidence," Jordan once said. He believed that excellence wasn't found in flash—it was forged in fundamentals. Even after winning multiple championships, he still trained like he was trying to make the team.

When asked about his competitive edge, Jordan never talked about natural ability. He talked about preparation. "Everybody has talent," he said. "But ability takes work." His off-season regimen was brutal. Strength training. Shooting mechanics. Mental visualization. He practiced harder than he played—because he believed the game was won before tip-off.

Michael Jordan didn't rise to greatness by accident. He built it—one disciplined repetition at a time. He reminds us that real men don't wait for the spotlight to shine. They train in the dark. They do the unglamorous work. They show up early, stay late, and master the basics when no one's watching.

Discipline doesn't always look heroic. But over time, it separates the committed from the casual. Just like it did with Jordan.

Discipline builds trust because it creates consistency. When a man's actions match his values—again and again—others feel safe around him. They know where he stands. They know he will follow through. Trust is earned not by grand declarations, but by small, repeated acts of integrity. That's what discipline makes possible.

David Goggins is a man who transformed his life through radical discipline. Once overweight, directionless, and working as a pest control technician, Goggins decided one day that enough was enough. He set his sights on becoming a Navy SEAL—one of the most grueling and selective paths in the military.

He failed. Then tried again. And again. On his third attempt, with broken bones and stress fractures, he passed. But that was just the beginning.

Since then, Goggins has become an ultramarathon runner, endurance athlete, and bestselling author. He's completed races most people wouldn't survive. But what sets him apart isn't just physical toughness—it's the mental discipline that drives him. He trains at 4 a.m., talks openly about doing the hard things he doesn't want to do, and created what he calls the "accountability mirror"—a brutal self-reflection practice where he forces himself to face his weaknesses daily.

Goggins says, "Discipline is about doing what you hate to do, but doing it like you love it." He doesn't chase comfort or applause. He chases growth. Every day.

His life is a walking reminder that discipline isn't a one-time act—it's a daily decision. And the man who masters discipline masters his future.

These men weren't born exceptional. They chose to train their minds, bodies, and behaviors. Not once—but daily. That consistency is what made them leaders. Their routines, their grit, and their refusal to let excuses win—that was their edge.

These acts were not random routines. They were foundations of greatness.

When a man shows up on time, keeps his word, and follows through—even in the small things—people begin to believe in him. It's not the loud declarations that earn confidence; it's the quiet follow-through. Discipline is what turns promises into patterns. Over time, that pattern becomes reliability. And reliability builds trust—in your home, your workplace, your friendships, and your leadership.

It doesn't mean rigidity—it means commitment. To your goals. To your growth. To your purpose.

Discipline is choosing what you want most over what you want now.

And when the world tempts you to take shortcuts, discipline reminds you: anything worth building takes work.

Discipline is your daily training ground. Step into it with resolve. Win the small battles. They shape the man you become.

When a man lives with discipline, people notice. They may not always say it—but they feel it. And that quiet consistency earns something you can't demand: respect.

TAKE ACTION ON THESE THREE CHALLENGES.

1. Reflect: Where are you undisciplined? Identify one area that needs consistency.
2. Act: Commit to one habit you will do every day this week—no exceptions.
3. Track: At the end of each day, journal how you felt after following through.

CHAPTER FIVE

RESPECT:
EARNING WHAT CANNOT BE DEMANDED

Respect is not given freely—it's earned. Not through force, not through fear, but through consistent character, clear communication, and a life lived with integrity. A man may gain compliance with power, but true respect? That can only be earned through presence, principle, and the way he makes others feel in his company.

Respect is the thread that weaves through every area of life. It affects how we lead, how we love, how we handle conflict, and how we carry ourselves. And just like faith, leadership, character, and discipline—it begins internally. Self-respect comes first.

A man who respects himself doesn't settle. He doesn't shrink to fit in. He doesn't betray his values to be accepted. He stands tall—not because he believes he's better than others, but because he knows he is responsible for living in alignment with his beliefs.

There's a story of a high school teacher who never raised his voice, never demanded attention, yet had full control of his classroom. When asked why his students respected him so much, he said, "Because I respect them first. I treat them how I expect them to treat me." His posture wasn't weakness—it was strength. His consistency earned authority.

Alexander the Great, though remembered as a fierce military commander, earned his soldiers' respect by marching beside them through snow, eating the same rations, and sleeping on the ground. His greatness wasn't just strategy—it was shared sacrifice. His men followed him across continents not just out of duty, but out of respect.

Respect isn't about titles. It's about how you treat people when no one's watching. Do you honor the janitor the same way you honor the CEO? Do you listen more than you talk? Do you keep your word even when it costs you?

It shows up in the little things: saying thank you. Making eye contact. Showing up on time. Returning what you borrowed. Owning your mistakes. In a world where disrespect has become common—where sarcasm is mistaken for strength and disregard for others is praised as boldness—men of respect stand out like lighthouses in a storm.

But respect isn't just about politeness. It's about presence. When you walk into a room, how do you carry yourself? Are you grounded? Are you aware of others? Are you honoring the space you occupy? People don't always remember your words—but they remember how you made them feel. That's the heart of respect.

Faith teaches us that every human being is created with inherent worth. Leadership calls us to serve, not dominate. Character keeps us honest. Discipline keeps us steady. And respect pulls it all together. It's the invisible force that allows relationships to thrive, teams to trust, and communities to grow.

Marcus Aurelius, the Roman emperor and Stoic philosopher, ruled with wisdom and humility. Despite his authority, he respected his people and advisors. His private writings show a man constantly checking his ego and choosing honor over hubris.

But respect isn't just about how we treat others. It's also about how we demand to be treated.

A man with no boundaries invites disrespect. But a man with quiet confidence, who values his time, voice, and values—he sets a tone. He doesn't have to yell. He doesn't have to threaten. He simply lives with such clarity and consistency that others recognize the standard.

George Washington led with restraint. After winning independence, he could have made himself king—but he stepped down, choosing the integrity of a republic over personal power. That act, more than any battle, earned him the enduring respect of a nation.

Respect also shows up in the way we handle disagreement. A respectful man doesn't need to win every argument. He listens. He speaks truth with grace. He lets others speak without needing to dominate the conversation. In today's divided world, this kind of respectful communication is rare—but powerful.

There's another story of a young manager who inherited a team twice his age. Instead of asserting dominance, he began by learning from each team member—asking for their input, honoring their experience, and valuing their perspective. Within months, the team didn't just comply—they rallied behind him. Why? Because he showed respect first.

In relationships, respect is the glue. Love without respect is manipulation. Friendship without respect is shallow. Partnership without respect is control. Whether you're dealing with your spouse, your children, your boss, or a stranger—respect sets the tone.

Keanu Reeves is one of the most recognizable actors in Hollywood, known for films like The Matrix and John Wick. But what has earned him deeper admiration is not just his talent—it's his consistent display of respect, humility, and kindness, even at the height of fame.

While many celebrities are known for ego or excess, Keanu lives modestly. He's been spotted giving up his seat on the subway, waiting in line like everyone else, and quietly donating millions to children's hospitals—without ever attaching his name to the headlines.

On set, crew members routinely praise him for remembering their names, treating everyone with equal respect, and thanking each team member individually after productions wrap. During the filming of The Matrix, he gifted a portion of his salary to the visual effects and costume teams—because he believed they were just as important to the film's success.

In interviews, he doesn't dominate conversations. He listens. He reflects. And he never talks down to anyone. He once said, "The simple act of paying attention can take you a long way."

Keanu reminds us that real respect isn't about grand gestures—
it's about daily posture. It's how you treat people when you don't
need anything from them. And in a world that often rewards
arrogance, his life is a quiet, unwavering example of masculine
respect in action.

In contrast, we've all seen leaders who bark orders, disrespect
time, or belittle others. They may get short-term results, but long-
term loyalty fades. Respect is the currency that lasts. It's not loud,
but it's powerful. And it echoes far beyond the moment.

In a world addicted to validation, respect is rare. But when a man
walks into a room and doesn't need approval—because he already
respects himself—people feel it. They notice. They remember.

Respect is never about ego. It's about value. Give it. Earn it.
Carry it.

True respect begins with how a man respects himself—and
nothing tests that more than how he handles what he feels. That's
where emotional strength comes in.

TAKE ACTION ON THESE THREE CHALLENGES.

1. Reflect: Are there areas of your life where you're tolerating disrespect—from others or from yourself?
2. Act: Choose one way to raise your standard this week—through boundaries, follow-through, or communication.
3. Extend: Show intentional respect to someone others often overlook. Watch how it shifts the dynamic.

CHAPTER SIX

EMOTIONAL STRENGTH:
THE POWER TO FEEL WITHOUT FOLDING

Not all strength can be seen. Some of the most powerful men in the world aren't the ones with the highest IQ—but the ones with the highest EQ: emotional intelligence. IQ measures logic, memory, and cognitive ability. It helps a man solve problems, plan, and strategize. But EQ? Emotional intelligence measures a man's ability to understand, regulate, and respond to emotions—his own and others'. And that's where emotional strength lives.

A man may be brilliant on paper, but if he can't handle stress, can't manage conflict, can't control his anger, or can't connect with those around him—his intelligence is incomplete. Emotional strength fills the gap. It's the power to remain grounded under pressure, composed in chaos, and connected in conflict.

It's the ability to stay present with your pain and patient with the pain of others. To feel deeply without falling apart. To lead with empathy, not ego. To protect with presence, not control. Emotional strength is not weakness—it's wisdom under fire.

It doesn't mean you never feel hurt, frustrated, afraid, or overwhelmed. It means you don't let those feelings define your behavior. Emotional strength is not the absence of feeling—it's the mastery of it.

Abraham Lincoln battled depression throughout his life. Yet he led a nation through civil war with empathy, patience, and wisdom.

Too often, men are taught that emotion is weakness. That tears are shameful. That silence is strength. But shutting down your emotions doesn't make you tough—it makes you numb. And numb men don't lead, love, or grow. They drift. They explode. Or they disappear when it matters most.

Emotional strength isn't about always having it together. It's about being honest with where you are and resilient enough to keep moving forward.

A firefighter once shared how he learned this the hard way. After responding to a tragic accident, he tried to "stay strong" by burying his feelings. But over time, the weight built up. His relationships suffered. His temper flared. Eventually, he broke down—not because he was weak, but because he hadn't let himself grieve. After getting help, he learned that real strength wasn't hiding his emotions. It was learning to process them with courage.

Emotional strength is knowing how to:

- Pause instead of react.
- Communicate instead of explode.
- Admit when you're hurting instead of pretending you're fine.
- Forgive instead of staying bitter.

It's in these decisions—not the big, flashy ones, but the quiet internal ones—where true strength is forged.

The strongest men in history weren't stone-faced. They were emotionally intelligent.

Terry Crews is best known today as a public personality—an energetic, muscular figure with a booming laugh. But behind the charisma is a man who has walked through deep emotional pain and chosen vulnerability over bravado.

Crews grew up in a household ruled by fear. His father was abusive, and Terry learned early on to mask his feelings and "man up" by hiding them. As he rose through his professional life, he carried that armor with him—on the outside, strong and successful. On the inside, struggling with anger, addiction, and shame.

Years later, he chose a different path. He opened up publicly about his emotional battles, his experiences with trauma, and how unresolved pain nearly cost him his marriage. He spoke out not with excuses—but with accountability. He sought therapy. He did the inner work. And he chose to tell the truth, even when it cost him comfort.

In his book Manhood, he writes, "Emotions don't make you weak. Ignoring them does."

Terry Crews reminds us that emotional strength isn't about suppressing pain—it's about facing it with courage. It takes real strength to break generational cycles, admit your faults, and fight for healing. And that kind of strength? That's what makes a man truly powerful.

Emotional strength doesn't mean being ruled by feelings. It means you own them—they don't own you.

Just like physical training builds muscle, emotional discipline builds maturity. And that's what separates men who survive from those who lead.

A man grounded in faith understands that emotions are part of creation—not flaws, but signals. Leadership built on trust requires emotional honesty. Character is tested in how we treat others when we're frustrated. Discipline includes managing moods, not just schedules. And respect begins with the courage to respect your own emotions before anyone else does.

Another man, a war veteran, once described how emotional strength saved his life. After years of suppressing pain and guilt, he joined a group of other vets who met weekly to talk—not just about war, but about life, family, fear, and loss. He said, "That group didn't just help me heal—it reminded me that I wasn't weak for feeling. I was human. And the strongest thing I ever did was show up."

In relationships, emotional strength is what allows a man to stay present when things get messy. To stay calm during a heated conversation. To listen even when his ego wants to defend. To remain steady—not stoic—when the people he loves are hurting.

We admire men who can lift heavy things. But we trust men who can handle emotional storms without retreating or attacking.

Here's the truth: emotional strength isn't natural. It's practiced. Grown and earned.

And it becomes the foundation for deeper connection, better leadership, and a life that doesn't collapse under pressure.

You don't need to be hard to be strong. You need to be whole. Let emotional strength become part of the man you're building.

Once a man learns to master his emotions instead of run from them, something powerful emerges: clarity. And clarity leads to purpose.

TAKE ACTION ON THESE THREE CHALLENGES.

1. Reflect: When was the last time you truly acknowledged your emotions instead of avoiding them?
2. Act: This week, open up to someone you trust about something real. Don't fix it. Just speak it.
3. Build: Choose one habit that strengthens your emotional health—journaling, therapy, prayer, or regular conversation with a friend.

CHAPTER SEVEN

PURPOSE:
THE FIRE THAT FUELS A MAN

Every man is born with a question burning inside him: *Why am I here?* It's not always asked out loud. But it's there—in the quiet frustration, the late-night overthinking, the restlessness even after reaching success. It's the deep hunger to be significant—to know your life counts for more than comfort, more than recognition. That it leaves a mark...

Purpose isn't something you stumble into. It's something you uncover, commit to, and grow through. It's the internal compass that keeps you moving when life doesn't go as planned. It's the fire that keeps you going when nothing else makes sense.

Without purpose, even strong men drift. They build things they don't care about. Chase things they don't value. Impress people they don't respect. But with purpose? A man becomes focused. Energized. Resilient.

A man working with purpose doesn't need constant motivation—he has clarity. He may get tired, but he doesn't quit. He doesn't need to be pushed. He's pulled forward by something bigger than himself.

Consider Viktor Frankl, a Holocaust survivor and psychiatrist. In the depths of a concentration camp, stripped of everything, he discovered that those who survived weren't necessarily the strongest—but those who had purpose. A reason to live. A reason to endure. He later wrote, "Those who have a why to live can bear almost any how."

Purpose doesn't mean having everything figured out. It means knowing what direction you're moving in and why it matters. It's what transforms work into calling, struggle into training, and pain into growth.

Just like faith centers a man, leadership expands his impact, character grounds him, discipline drives him, respect guides his relationships, and emotional strength sustains his presence—purpose gives all of them context. It answers the question: *What is all this for?*

Purpose is found at the intersection of three things:

- What you love.
- What you're good at.
- What the world needs from you.

It's not always a job. Sometimes it's fatherhood. Sometimes it's mentorship. Sometimes it's building something that will outlast you.

There's a story of a man who spent twenty years working a high-powered corporate job. He had money, status, and connections—but every morning felt like a burden. One day he volunteered at a weekend camp for foster kids, just to help out. Something clicked. That weekend led to monthly service, then a full-time shift into nonprofit work. He didn't make as much—but he never felt more alive. That's purpose.

Purpose doesn't always come in a flash of lightning. Sometimes it's a whisper. A tug. A persistent call that won't leave you alone. The key is to stop ignoring it.

Every man is born with purpose. But many never uncover it—lost in distraction, dulled by doubt, or chasing what doesn't satisfy.

Here's the truth: you don't find purpose by waiting. You find it by moving. By doing. By testing. By failing. By paying attention to what lights you up and what breaks your heart.

Elon Musk isn't known for playing it safe. From launching rockets with SpaceX to revolutionizing electric vehicles with Tesla, Musk has consistently chased bold, purpose-driven goals that most people called impossible.

He's faced failure, ridicule, near-bankruptcy, and massive public pressure—but purpose has always fueled his decisions. Musk once said, "I think it is possible for ordinary people to choose to be extraordinary." For him, that choice has always been tied to solving humanity's biggest challenges—whether that means making sustainable energy mainstream or colonizing Mars.

In 2008, both Tesla and SpaceX were nearly bankrupt. He invested his last remaining funds between the two companies to keep them alive. That's not business strategy—that's purpose on display. He didn't just want to build companies. He wanted to change the future.

Musk works 80–100 hour weeks, not for ego, but for impact. He's deeply involved in product design, engineering, and long-term strategy. He doesn't chase balance—he chases mission.

Elon Musk reminds us that purpose isn't always comfortable. Sometimes it looks like criticism, sacrifice, and sleepless nights. But when you're living for something bigger than yourself, the obstacles become fuel—not excuses.

When you live with purpose:

- Your time matters more.
- Your relationships deepen.
- Your energy becomes focused.
- Your legacy becomes intentional.

And when you die—and you will—people won't remember your bank account or your resume. They'll remember your impact. They'll feel what you gave. They'll carry what you built.

That's purpose.

Don't just exist. Build something. Become something. Leave something. Let purpose be your fuel.

Purpose is powerful—but no man can live it out alone. To build something that lasts, you need brothers who walk with you, sharpen you, and challenge you to stay the course.

TAKE ACTION ON THESE THREE CHALLENGES.

1. Reflect: What makes you feel most alive? What do you do that others thank you for?
2. Act: Take one step this week toward something that aligns with your purpose—no matter how small.
3. Ask: What breaks your heart? What makes you angry for the right reasons? Let that guide where you serve.

CHAPTER EIGHT

BROTHERHOOD:
THE STRENGTH OF STANDING TOGETHER

No man becomes great alone. Behind every strong man is a circle—brothers, mentors, friends—men who sharpen him, support him, challenge him, and walk with him through fire. Brotherhood isn't a luxury. It's a necessity.

Modern culture tells us to go it alone. That real strength is self-made. That needing others is weakness. But that's a lie. Isolation may protect your ego, but it starves your soul. A man without brotherhood is like a soldier without a unit—vulnerable, exposed, and likely to fall under pressure.

Brotherhood doesn't mean having a crowd. It means having a few men you trust with your truth. Men who see your blind spots, hold you accountable, speak life into you, and stand with you when life hits hard.

Think of the Navy SEALs. Their entire strength lies in their trust. Each man knows the man beside him is ready to fight, protect, and sacrifice. Their bond isn't just training—it's blood, sweat, and absolute loyalty. That's brotherhood.

Travis Manion and Brendan Looney met as roommates at the U.S. Naval Academy in 2001. Both were standout athletes—Travis a wrestler, Brendan a football player who later switched to lacrosse. Their shared commitment to service, discipline, and excellence forged a deep friendship that transcended the typical college bond.

They were known for their competitive spirit, constantly pushing each other to be better, whether in the gym or in their studies. Yet, beneath the rivalry was a profound respect and loyalty. They referred to themselves as "brothers from another mother," a testament to the strength of their connection.

After graduation in 2004, their paths diverged—Travis commissioned as a Marine officer, Brendan as a Navy intelligence officer. Despite the distance, their bond remained unshaken.

In 2007, Travis was killed by a sniper in Iraq while leading his Marines during a patrol. His death deeply affected Brendan, who honored his friend's memory by wearing a bracelet engraved with Travis's name during his deployments.

Brendan went on to become a Navy SEAL, exemplifying the same courage and dedication that had defined his friend's life. In 2010, during his deployment in Afghanistan, Brendan was killed in a helicopter crash.

Recognizing the depth of their friendship, Brendan's family requested that he be buried beside Travis at Arlington National Cemetery. Today, their graves lie side by side—a powerful symbol of brotherhood that endures beyond life.

Their story reminds us that brotherhood is not just about shared experiences, but about unwavering support, sacrifice, and love that transcends even death.

Throughout history, great men didn't walk alone. In Scripture, even the mightiest had brothers. Moses had Aaron—not just a sibling, but a partner in calling. David had Jonathan, a friend whose loyalty ran deeper than blood. Jesus chose twelve men to walk beside him, not because he needed numbers, but because he knew the mission required community.

In ancient Greece, warriors fought in tight phalanx formations, shields locked together—each man's life protected not by his own strength, but by the discipline and courage of the one beside him. In the Roman legions, it wasn't just weapons or numbers that won battles—it was the unbreakable loyalty and trust between brothers-in-arms that often turned the tide of war.

In the American abolitionist movement, Frederick Douglass didn't fight alone. Men like William Lloyd Garrison, and later, black intellectual allies such as Martin Delany and Charles Remond, stood with him when it was dangerous to do so. Their unity turned personal conviction into national momentum.

Across cultures and continents—from the samurai brotherhoods of feudal Japan to the warrior tribes of Africa—true strength has always come in groups of men bound by shared mission, trust, and sacrifice. Brotherhood has shaped revolutions, rebuilt nations, and restored the broken-hearted.

Wherever men stood for something greater than themselves, they did it with others at their side. Brotherhood has never been about comfort. It's always been about commitment.

Brotherhood shows up in a father who checks on his son's friends. In a friend who calls you out when you're drifting. In a mentor who refuses to let you settle. It's the quiet man who shows up to help you move, drive you to a funeral, or sit in silence when words aren't enough.

We all want to be the man others count on. But first—we need to be the man who admits he needs others too.

A construction worker once shared how he was struggling through divorce. He was showing up to work, wearing a smile, but falling apart inside. One day, a coworker who barely said much handed him coffee and said, "You don't have to carry this alone." That simple act cracked the wall. They started meeting before shifts just to talk. It saved him. Not because of deep wisdom. But because of presence.

Brotherhood heals.

You need men who:

- Call you out when you're wrong.
- Call you up when you forget who you are.
- Carry you when you can't walk alone.

Brotherhood isn't soft. It's steel. It's forged in trust, truth, and time.

You don't need 100 friends. You need 2 or 3 real ones. Men who have your back and remind you who you are when life tries to convince you otherwise.

Strong men build strong circles. They know that iron sharpens iron, and that the strength of a man is often revealed by the strength of the men he surrounds himself with. These men don't compete—they complete. They're not intimidated by another man's greatness—they amplify it.

They don't gather just to kill time. They gather to build something—character, discipline, legacy. They push each other in the gym, in business, in marriage, and in faith. When one falls, the others lift. When one wins, the others celebrate. When one wanders, the others go after him.

They don't waste time with gossip or games. They speak truth, even when it stings. They show up even when it's inconvenient. Loyalty, not convenience, defines their bond.

They don't just share wins—they share battles. They share late-night doubts, early-morning prayers, difficult conversations, and relentless accountability. They challenge laziness, confront excuses, and refuse to let each other stay stuck.

In these circles, mediocrity doesn't survive. Growth becomes the standard. Brotherhood becomes the fuel. They celebrate. They mourn. They fight for one another.

If you want to build true brotherhood, start by showing up as your authentic self. Be a Real Man—not one who leads with ego or appearance, but with honesty and integrity. Don't hide behind silence, sarcasm, or surface talk. Speak truth. Be present. Brotherhood isn't something you stumble into. It's forged by men with the courage to go first.

Be the one who reaches out. Be the one who checks in. Be the one who doesn't let silence win. Be the Real Man who chooses connection over comfort, and responsibility over retreat.

Strong men build strong circles. And Real Men build them on trust, truth, and time.

So, drop the mask. Lose the ego. Speak truth. Show up and keep showing up.

Because no man rises alone. And no man heals alone either.

Brotherhood doesn't just make life lighter—it makes you stronger. Build it. Protect it. Be it.

Brotherhood gives a man strength—but at the end of the day, courage is personal. It's the decision to stand, even when you stand alone.

TAKE ACTION ON THESE THREE CHALLENGES.

1. Reflect: Who are the men in your life who make you better? Do they know it?
2. Act: Reach out to one man this week and speak life into him. Start the conversation.
3. Build: If you don't have that circle—create it. Start small. Start real. Just start.

CHAPTER NINE

COURAGE:
DOING WHAT'S RIGHT EVEN WHEN IT'S HARD

Courage isn't the absence of fear—it's the decision to act in spite of it. Every man faces moments where fear tries to take the lead. Sometimes it shows up as hesitation. Sometimes as silence. Sometimes as avoidance. But in every case, courage is the turning point. It's the moment that defines the man.

We often think of courage as battlefield valor or heroic rescues. But courage also looks like telling the truth when it's easier to lie. Walking away from a toxic job or relationship. Standing alone for what's right when everyone else stays quiet. Real courage is quiet, firm, and deeply personal.

History is built on the backs of courageous men.

Winston Churchill stood alone against the Nazi tide while Europe crumbled. He didn't wait for consensus—he spoke conviction. Despite criticism, pressure, and the looming shadow of defeat, he stood in front of a broken nation and said, "We shall never surrender."

John Adams, one of America's founding fathers, showed immense courage when he defended British soldiers involved in the Boston Massacre. Though deeply unpopular, he believed in justice and the rule of law. His decision cost him favor and friends, but it preserved the moral foundation of the country he would help build.

Adams once said, "Facts are stubborn things," and his actions proved that courage often means standing for truth even when the crowd stands against you.

During the Montgomery Bus Boycott, it wasn't just Martin Luther King Jr. who showed courage—it was the thousands of unknown men who walked miles to work each day, risking jobs and safety to stand for dignity.

And in Tiananmen Square, the unnamed "Tank Man" didn't speak a word. He didn't hold a sign. He just stood in the street— one man in front of a column of tanks. No weapons. No crowd. Just courage.

These stories remind us that courage doesn't always roar. Sometimes it's a whisper that says, "I will not back down today."

Courage is needed now more than ever. Not just in protests or politics—but in our homes, relationships, and daily lives.

You need courage to:

- Apologize first.
- Forgive someone who won't say sorry.
- Ask for help when your pride wants to hide.
- Speak your truth when your voice shakes.
- Make a hard decision because it's right—not easy.

Courage is what turns values into actions. It's what moves a man from belief to behavior.

Without courage, faith becomes routine. Leadership becomes performative. Character becomes flexible. Discipline becomes conditional. Respect becomes selective. Brotherhood becomes shallow. Purpose becomes theoretical. And emotional strength becomes a script.

With courage? Everything becomes real.

Hamdi Ulukaya was born into a Kurdish dairy-farming family in eastern Turkey. Facing political oppression and limited opportunities, he immigrated to the United States in the 1990s with little money and limited English proficiency. Settling in upstate New York, he initially started a modest feta cheese business.

In 2005, Ulukaya came across a defunct yogurt factory that had been closed by Kraft Foods. Despite lacking formal business training and facing skepticism from advisors, he took a bold risk by purchasing the facility. Drawing from his heritage, he introduced a Mediterranean-style strained yogurt to the American market, branding it as Chobani, meaning "shepherd" in Turkish.

Ulukaya's journey was fraught with challenges. He invested his savings, worked tirelessly to perfect the product, and faced stiff competition from established brands. Yet, his unwavering commitment paid off. Within five years, Chobani became the top-selling yogurt brand in the U.S., revolutionizing the industry.

Beyond business success, Ulukaya demonstrated moral courage. He implemented progressive workplace policies, including generous employee benefits and profit-sharing. In 2016, he surprised employees by granting them a 10% stake in the company. Moreover, as a vocal advocate for refugees, he pledged significant portions of his wealth to support displaced communities and hired numerous refugees at Chobani facilities.

Hamdi Ulukaya's story teaches us that courage isn't just about bold decisions—it's about standing firm in one's values, taking risks for a greater good, and leading with compassion and integrity.

Courage is a skill. It's a muscle. The more you use it, the stronger it gets. Every hard conversation you don't avoid, every fear you face instead of fleeing, every small stand you take—it adds to your foundation. And over time, your threshold for fear lowers, and your instinct to act strengthens.

It begins in everyday decisions. Waking up and showing up when your mind says stay down. Admitting a mistake at work instead of covering it up. Saying no to peer pressure even when you'll be mocked. These aren't grand gestures—but they're training ground for the bigger battles.

Men who consistently exercise courage build a presence that others trust. They become anchors in uncertain times. They don't need to posture. Their track record speaks.

And the more you model it, the more others rise around you. Courage creates ripple effects. It raises the bar in your circle, in your home, in your workplace. One act of courage can unlock someone else's.

Like the teacher who reported corruption in his school district, even when his job was on the line. Or the father who broke generational patterns by choosing to raise his kids with patience instead of anger. They weren't trying to be heroes. They were just doing what was right—again and again.

That's how courage is built. That's how courage leads.

Courage isn't the absence of fear. It's the commitment to stand, speak, and act when it counts.

Be the man who does what's right—even when it's hard.

Courage isn't just about what you fight for today—it's about who and what you fight for tomorrow. And nowhere is that truer than in fatherhood.

TAKE ACTION ON THESE THREE CHALLENGES.

1. Reflect: Where in your life are you avoiding action out of fear?
2. Act: Do one thing this week that scares you but aligns with your values.
3. Lead: Share a moment of courage from your past with someone younger than you. Let it spark theirs.

CHAPTER TEN

FATHERHOOD:
RAISING THE FUTURE, ONE DECISION AT A TIME

Fatherhood isn't just a role—it's a mission. It's one of the highest forms of leadership, sacrifice, and influence a man can take on. And yet, it's one of the least celebrated. Too often, fathers are reduced to stereotypes: the absent one, the angry one, the clueless one. But strong fathers are nation-builders. Legacy-makers. And their impact echoes for generations.

A father sets the tone of a home. His words carry weight. His example shape's identity. He teaches—through presence, protection, correction, and consistency. When a father shows up, the ground feels more stable beneath a child's feet.

You don't have to be perfect to be a good father. But you do have to be present.

There's a story of a truck driver who worked long hours, barely scraping by. But every night, no matter how tired he was, he sat at the table with his kids and asked how their day was. He made them feel seen. Heard. Loved. None of them remember the trucks he drove. But they remember his voice, his laugh, his steadiness.

That's fatherhood.

In history, we find men who understood the generational weight of being a father—even if they weren't famous for it. Benjamin Franklin, one of the wisest minds of his time, understood the weight of fatherhood—not just through his children, but through the legacy of wisdom, civic responsibility, and character he passed down. His letters to his son and grandson reveal a man deeply invested in shaping future generations.

Theodore Roosevelt, after losing his wife and mother on the same day, still prioritized his children. He took them on adventures, wrote them letters, and remained a consistent part of their lives—even as president.

General Douglas MacArthur once wrote a prayer for his son, asking not for success or fame, but for strength, humility, and moral courage. He understood that what he passed down mattered more than what he achieved.

Fatherhood isn't always biological. Coaches, mentors, uncles, and men who step in to guide, protect, and invest—they too carry the spirit of a father. What matters most is not bloodline, but backbone.

Strong fathers:

- Lead with patience, not intimidation.
- Discipline with love, not rage.
- Listen more than they lecture.
- Protect without smothering.
- Prepare their children to rise, not rely.

Children raised by strong fathers grow up with deeper confidence, greater emotional security, and a stronger sense of resilience.

But make no mistake—fatherhood is hard. It demands everything. Time. Energy. Selflessness. And above all, consistency.

Being a father means going to work even when you're tired. Having tough conversations when you'd rather avoid them. Apologizing when you've messed up. And showing up—day after day—because your presence is the most powerful gift you'll ever give.

And yes, fatherhood requires courage. To break cycles you grew up with. To raise kids in a chaotic world. To admit when you don't have all the answers—but stay anyway.

The most powerful fathers are not the loudest. They're the ones who build quietly, faithfully, intentionally.

David A. Hirsch is a businessman and philanthropist who has dedicated his life to promoting responsible fatherhood. In 1997, recognizing the critical role fathers play in the lives of their children, he founded the Illinois Fatherhood Initiative, the nation's first statewide nonprofit fatherhood organization. His mission was clear: to combat father absence and encourage men to be active, present, and engaged fathers.

Hirsch's commitment deepened when he established the 21st Century Dads Foundation, which includes programs like the Special Fathers Network—a mentoring initiative for fathers raising children with special needs. Through this network, experienced fathers provide support and guidance to those navigating the unique challenges of parenting children with disabilities.

As a father of five, Hirsch understands the complexities and rewards of fatherhood firsthand. He has authored the book 21st Century Dads: A Father's Journey to Break the Cycle of Father Absence, sharing insights and stories to inspire and equip other fathers. Additionally, he hosts the Special Fathers Network Dad to Dad Podcast, featuring conversations with fathers from diverse backgrounds who share their experiences and wisdom.

David A. Hirsch's work underscores the transformative power of fatherhood. His efforts have not only impacted individual families but have also contributed to a broader cultural shift, emphasizing the importance of active and engaged fathers in building strong, healthy communities.

When a man embraces fatherhood as a calling, he sees every conversation, every hug, every correction, and every moment of presence as part of a greater mission—not to control his children, but to equip them. To lead them. To prepare them for a world that will test everything he teaches at home.

Fatherhood isn't a title. It's a calling. Titles can be given. Callings must be answered—over and over again. Anyone can become a father biologically, but it takes a man of grit, heart, and discipline to truly live out what it means to be a father day in and day out. A title might earn a man recognition, but a calling demands his life. It pulls him out of selfishness and into service. It challenges him to become more than he was yesterday—because someone else is watching, learning, and becoming through his example.

A calling doesn't clock out. It doesn't wait until it's convenient. It keeps showing up, especially when it's hard. And it transforms a man in the process.

In the end, the legacy of a father isn't measured by what he leaves behind—but by who he raises up.

Fatherhood is where legacy begins—not in what you leave behind, but in who you raise up every day.

TAKE ACTION ON THESE THREE CHALLENGES.

1. Reflect: Are you being the man you want your children—or future children—to model?
2. Act: Choose one moment this week to engage with your children more deeply—without distractions.
3. Build: Identify one pattern from your own upbringing that you want to stop or strengthen. Take action.

CHAPTER ELEVEN

LEGACY:
WHAT YOU LEAVE BEHIND SPEAKS LOUDER THAN YOU

Every man leaves a legacy—whether intentional or accidental. The question is never *if* you'll leave one, but *what kind* you'll leave. Legacy isn't built in a moment. It's built in every decision, every conversation, every sacrifice, and every stand.

Legacy is not about what you accomplish. It's about what you instill in others. Your kids. Your friends. Your team. Your community. It's not what people say about you when you're in the room. It's what continues long after you're gone.

We live in a world obsessed with temporary wins—money, status, likes, followers. But the men who truly shape the future are the ones who think beyond themselves. They live with the end in mind, not in fear—but with purpose. With clarity. With discipline.

Legacy starts small. A boy watches how his father talks to his mother. A young man remembers how his coach corrected him without shaming him. A team watches how their leader handles defeat without blaming everyone else. These moments echo far beyond the moment.

History is full of men who built legacy through how they lived, not just what they built.

Nelson Mandela chose forgiveness over vengeance, and helped unite a nation still raw with pain. His legacy wasn't just political—it was moral.

John Wooden, the legendary UCLA basketball coach, didn't just create champions—he created men of integrity. His Pyramid of Success was more than a strategy—it was a philosophy that shaped lives long after the buzzer.

Jackie Robinson endured hate, threats, and isolation—not just to play baseball, but to break barriers. His courage became a bridge for others.

These men weren't perfect. But they lived with vision. With principle. With the understanding that how you live matters just as much—if not more—than what you achieve.

Legacy is built:

- When you raise your children with truth, love, and consistency.
- When you invest in others who may never repay you.
- When you choose discipline over distraction.
- When you speak life instead of gossip.
- When you live your values even when no one sees.

You don't have to be rich to leave a legacy. You don't need a title. You need clarity, conviction, and the daily commitment to become a man worth remembering.

Yvon Chouinard, founder of the outdoor apparel company Patagonia, has redefined what it means to leave a legacy in the business world. An accomplished climber and environmentalist, Chouinard started by crafting climbing gear for himself and his friends, leading to the establishment of Patagonia in 1973.

Under his leadership, Patagonia became known not just for high-quality products but also for its unwavering commitment to environmental and social responsibility. Chouinard implemented groundbreaking initiatives, such as donating 1% of sales to environmental causes and ensuring fair labor practices throughout the supply chain.

In 2022, taking an unprecedented step, Chouinard transferred ownership of Patagonia to a trust and nonprofit organization, ensuring that all profits are used to combat climate change and protect undeveloped land globally. This move solidified his dedication to the planet and set a new standard for corporate philanthropy.

Yvon Chouinard's story teaches us that legacy isn't solely about personal success or wealth accumulation—it's about making enduring contributions that benefit future generations and the world at large. His actions challenge us to consider how our choices today shape the legacy we leave behind.

Legacy isn't about leaving behind wealth. It's about leaving behind wisdom. A way of living. A standard. A name that carries weight not because it was loud—but because it was consistent, strong, and deeply rooted in purpose.

One man told his grandson, "You carry my last name. Make sure it means something when you say it." That's legacy.

And the truth is, your legacy isn't just about the people you know. It's about the ripple effect you create through those you impact. Someone is always watching. Learning. Absorbing who you are—so they can become who they need to be.

Everything we've discussed in this book—faith, leadership, character, discipline, respect, emotional strength, purpose, brotherhood, courage, fatherhood, and service—all of it stacks into one thing: the legacy you leave behind.

Legacy is what others carry because of you. But it starts with what you carry within. And that comes down to the hardest work of all: mastering yourself.

Because in the end, your legacy is not what you leave *to* people. It's what you leave *in* them.

TAKE ACTION ON THESE THREE CHALLENGES.

1. Reflect: If your life ended today, what would people say you stood for?
2. Act: Choose one behavior this week that reflects the legacy you want to leave.
3. Build: Write down your values. Live them. Let them guide every decision from this point forward.

CHAPTER TWELVE

SELF-MASTERY:
THE DAILY PURSUIT OF THE MAN WITHIN

The hardest man you'll ever lead is yourself.

Self-mastery is the quiet war fought behind closed doors. It's the discipline to choose growth over comfort, vision over impulse, truth over excuses. It's not perfection—but the relentless pursuit of becoming the man you know you're meant to be.

In a world built to distract, delay, and divide, mastering yourself is a radical act. It's easier to point fingers, shift blame, or wait for permission. But real men take ownership. They take inventory. They take action.

Self-mastery isn't about control—it's about alignment. When your thoughts, actions, habits, and values all point in the same direction, power multiplies. Clarity deepens. Momentum builds.

Every chapter in this book rests on this one principle: if you can't lead yourself, you can't lead others.

Kobe Bryant, known as the "Black Mamba," didn't just rely on talent. He was relentless—starting workouts at 4 a.m., obsessively studying game tapes, and turning even practices into pressure-cooked tests of will. His excellence wasn't given—it was earned, one brutal rep at a time.

Self-mastery isn't glamorous. It's not exciting. But it builds everything else. It makes you a man people trust, follow, depend on. A man whose words match his walk.

Jocko Willink is a retired U.S. Navy SEAL officer who has become a prominent advocate for self-discipline and leadership. During his 20-year military career, he served as the commander of SEAL Team 3's Task Unit Bruiser in the Iraq War, leading some of the most intense combat operations in the Battle of Ramadi. His leadership and valor earned him the Silver Star and Bronze Star medals.

After retiring from the Navy, Willink co-founded Echelon Front, a leadership consulting firm, and authored several books, including Extreme Ownership and Discipline Equals Freedom. These works emphasize the importance of taking full responsibility for one's actions and the role of discipline in achieving personal and professional success.

Willink's daily routine reflects his commitment to self-mastery. He rises at 4:30 a.m. every day to engage in rigorous physical training, a habit he developed during his military service. This early start allows him to maintain focus and productivity throughout his day, managing various ventures including his podcast, consulting firm, and supplement line.

He advocates for the principle that discipline leads to freedom, suggesting that by exercising control over one's actions and decisions, individuals can achieve greater autonomy and success in life. Willink's teachings have inspired many to adopt a disciplined approach to personal development and leadership.

Jocko Willink's journey illustrates that self-mastery involves a relentless commitment to discipline, responsibility, and continuous improvement. His life serves as a testament to the power of taking ownership and striving for excellence in all endeavors.

These and countless men you'll never hear about wake up every day, push past their excuses, and do the right thing again and again. They don't get praise—but they live with peace, clarity, and earned confidence.

Self-mastery includes:

- Managing your time like it matters—because it does.
- Guarding your inputs—what you watch, read, listen to.
- Monitoring your thoughts and language.
- Holding yourself accountable—no one else will.
- Reflecting daily—so you stay aligned with who you say you are.

It's the gym when you're tired. The hard conversation when you'd rather scroll. The extra 15 minutes of focus when your brain says quit. The honest look in the mirror at what's working—and what's not.

He becomes unshakable not because life gets easier, but because he gets stronger. The man who masters himself can't be easily manipulated, thrown off course, or broken by hardship. He leads not with ego, but with clarity. Because the war within is the war that determines everything else.

Master that—and you can handle anything.

Jim Stovall is an American author, entrepreneur, and motivational speaker who exemplifies the essence of self-mastery. At the age of 29, Stovall lost his sight due to a degenerative eye disease. Rather than succumbing to despair, he transformed this personal adversity into a catalyst for growth and contribution.

Recognizing the lack of accessible media for the visually impaired, Stovall founded the Narrative Television Network, which makes television and movies accessible to blind and visually impaired individuals by unobtrusively adding the voice of a narrator to the existing soundtrack. His commitment to inclusivity and empowerment has earned him numerous accolades, including an Emmy Award and recognition as the International Humanitarian of the Year.

Beyond his entrepreneurial ventures, Stovall authored the bestselling book The Ultimate Gift, which was later adapted into a feature film. Through his writings and speeches, he shares insights on overcoming challenges, embracing change, and harnessing inner strength.

Jim Stovall's journey illustrates that self-mastery involves transforming personal challenges into opportunities for growth and service. His life serves as a testament to the power of resilience, purpose, and unwavering determination.

The man who masters himself isn't perfect. He still stumbles, still feels doubt, still gets tired. But he doesn't let those moments define him. He learns. He adjusts. He sharpens. His strength isn't found in never failing—it's in refusing to stay down. He doesn't seek applause for his efforts; his reward is inner peace, quiet confidence, and knowing he's moving in the right direction.

You don't drift into greatness. You decide into it. Then you prove it—daily.

Self-mastery sharpens your edge—but what happens when life hits back? That's where resilience proves what's real.

TAKE ACTION ON THESE THREE CHALLENGES.

1. Reflect: What area of your life are you most inconsistent in—and why?
2. Act: Choose one habit to track for the next 30 days. Stay with it.
3. Sharpen: Find a brother who will hold you accountable and challenge you to level up.

CHAPTER THIRTEEN

RESILIENCE:
GETTING BACK UP STRONGER THAN BEFORE

Every man gets knocked down. By failure. By betrayal. By heartbreak, loss, exhaustion, or setbacks that blindside him when he least expects it. But what defines a Real Man isn't that he avoids the fall—it's how he rises.

Resilience is the muscle that makes rising possible. It's the strength to absorb the hit, process the pain, learn the lesson, and keep moving forward—wiser, sharper, and more dangerous in the best way. It doesn't mean pretending you're okay. It means refusing to stay down.

The world will test you. That's a promise. But the outcome is up to you.

History remembers men who refused to fold.

Walt Disney was fired from a newspaper job for "lacking imagination." He could've stopped there, convinced the world didn't see his value. But he kept creating. He launched Laugh-O-Gram Studios, which quickly went bankrupt, leaving him with nothing but debt and a suitcase of drawings. Still, he didn't quit.

He hopped on a train to California with $40 in his pocket and a dream that hadn't died. He faced rejection after rejection while trying to sell his ideas. Even when his character Oswald the Lucky Rabbit was stolen from him by his own distributor, he didn't crumble. Instead, he invented someone better: Mickey Mouse.

From there, Disney's setbacks became his sharpening stone. He pioneered synchronized sound in animation, pushed for full-length animated films when critics laughed, and risked everything to build Disneyland—a project many called a foolish fantasy. But he saw something bigger, and he had the resilience to keep going until it became reality.

Today, his vision has shaped global culture—not because he avoided failure, but because he refused to be defined by it.

Thomas Edison failed over a thousand times while inventing the light bulb. When asked how it felt to fail so many times, he said, "I have not failed. I've just found 10,000 ways that won't work." But one of his greatest tests came not in the lab—but in the fire.

In 1914, Edison's laboratory caught fire and burned to the ground. Years of research, prototypes, and records—all gone in hours. He watched the flames with his son beside him. When the boy began to panic, Edison calmly said, "Go get your mother. She'll never see anything like this again."

Instead of collapsing into defeat, Edison began rebuilding immediately. The next morning, walking through the ashes, he said, "There is great value in disaster. All our mistakes are burned up. Thank God we can start anew." That kind of mindset is resilience in its purest form. Edison didn't let the fire define him—he used it as fuel.

He went on to invent even more and filed over 1,000 patents in his lifetime. His legacy wasn't just innovation—it was unbreakable grit."

Resilient men don't just survive. They adapt. They evolve. They come back stronger.

Resilience isn't about ignoring pain. It's about converting it. It's:

- Choosing discipline over despair.
- Turning failure into feedback.
- Turning wounds into wisdom.
- Choosing to build when others would break.

Resilience lives in the single dad who rebuilds his life for his kids. In the entrepreneur who gets denied 50 times but pitches again. In the man who fights through addiction and shows up to his recovery meeting every week. In the athlete who rehabs for months to step back onto the field.

Resilience is also in the mundane: Waking up and trying again. Saying sorry when it hurts. Starting over when no one claps. It's not always flashy—but it's always powerful.

And resilience compounds. Every time you get up, you build grit. Every time you learn from the loss, you level up. Every time you finish what you started, even when it's hard, you remind yourself: I am still here.

Faith gives you something to hold onto. Character helps you endure with integrity. Discipline keeps you steady. Emotional strength helps you process and respond. Brotherhood reminds you you're not alone. But resilience is the thread that pulls it all forward when life tries to hold you back.

Resilience isn't about how hard you fall. It's about how deeply you rise.

Get up. Again. And again. That's how real men are forged.

Resilience keeps you standing. But now it's time to walk with purpose. Because your life isn't just about surviving—it's about living on mission.

TAKE ACTION ON THESE THREE CHALLENGES.

1. Reflect: What past setback has shaped you most—and what did it teach you?
2. Act: Choose one unfinished task or goal and commit to finishing it this month.
3. Remind: Speak this to yourself daily: *"I've been hit before. I'll rise again."*

CHAPTER FOURTEEN

MISSION:
LIVING FOR SOMETHING GREATER THAN YOURSELF

Every man needs a mission. Not just a job. Not just a goal. A mission. Something bigger than comfort. Bigger than ego. Bigger than his personal success.

Mission gives your life a trajectory. It points your energy toward purpose. It keeps you locked in when others quit. It gets you out of bed on the hard days. And it gives meaning to the storms you've survived.

The most dangerous man isn't the one who's angry. It's the one who's focused. Who knows why he's here, who he's becoming, and what he refuses to back down from.

Men without mission drift. They chase money, validation, short-term highs. They settle for busy instead of becoming. They numb the pain of aimlessness with distraction, addiction, or comfort. But men with mission move differently. They don't have time to play small. Their steps are heavier, because every step is tied to something eternal.

Think of Ernest Shackleton, the polar explorer. His ship was trapped and crushed in Antarctic ice. With no chance of rescue, he led his crew of 27 men on a near-impossible survival journey across brutal seas. Not a single man died. Why? Because Shackleton never lost the mission: get every man home. His focus, resolve, and daily leadership turned a tragedy into a triumph.

Another example: Neil Armstrong, the first man to walk on the moon. His mission wasn't just about exploration—it was about proving what was possible. With the eyes of the world on him and the pressure of an entire nation behind him, he stayed calm, focused, and committed. His iconic step onto the lunar surface wasn't just the result of science—it was the result of discipline, teamwork, and a man who never lost sight of the mission entrusted to him. "One small step for man," he said, but it symbolized a giant leap driven by courage and clarity.

A mission doesn't have to be massive to be meaningful. Some of the most powerful missions are deeply personal:

- Raising your children with intention.
- Breaking a generational curse.
- Building a business that puts people before profit.
- Mentoring younger men so they don't make the mistakes you did.
- Using your pain to protect someone else from theirs.

Brett Hagler is a social entrepreneur who transformed a personal mission into a global movement to end homelessness. In 2014, after witnessing the dire housing conditions in Haiti, Hagler co-founded New Story, a nonprofit organization dedicated to providing safe and sustainable homes for families in need.

Under his leadership, New Story has built over 2,000 homes across countries like Haiti, El Salvador, and Mexico. Notably, the organization partnered with ICON, a construction technologies company, to create the world's first 3D-printed community in Nacajuca, Mexico. This innovative approach significantly reduces construction time and costs, making housing more accessible to impoverished communities.

Hagler's mission extends beyond building homes; it's about restoring dignity and hope to those who have been marginalized. By leveraging technology and innovative partnerships, he has redefined what's possible in humanitarian efforts.

Brett Hagler's journey illustrates that a clear and compassionate mission can drive groundbreaking solutions to some of the world's most pressing problems. His work serves as a testament to the power of aligning personal purpose with impactful action.

Mission isn't about size—it's about significance.

Your mission defines your values. Shapes your schedule. Clarifies your circle. And reveals your next right step, even when the road is dark.

Blake Mycoskie, an American entrepreneur, revolutionized the concept of social entrepreneurship by founding TOMS Shoes in 2006. Inspired by a trip to Argentina where he witnessed the hardships faced by children without shoes, Mycoskie launched a company with a simple yet powerful mission: for every pair of shoes sold, a new pair would be given to a child in need.

This "One for One" model not only addressed immediate needs but also set a precedent for integrating social causes into business strategies. Under Mycoskie's leadership, TOMS expanded its mission to include eyewear, providing vision care to those in need, coffee, and supporting clean water initiatives in developing countries.

Beyond product sales, Mycoskie authored Start Something That Matters, sharing his journey and encouraging others to pursue meaningful work. He also committed to donating 100% of the book's royalties to support social entrepreneurs.

Blake Mycoskie's story illustrates that aligning business objectives with a clear social mission can drive both commercial success and global impact, inspiring a new generation of entrepreneurs to prioritize purpose alongside profit.

You won't always feel motivated. That's normal. But a man on a mission doesn't wait for motivation. He moves with discipline, purpose, and focus—especially when it's hard. Especially when no one's watching.

Your mission might evolve over time. That's okay. But the key is to never live without one.

Remember, your mission makes every other chapter in this book matter:

- Faith grounds your mission.
- Leadership executes it.
- Character proves it.
- Discipline fuels it.
- Respect earns trust in it.

- Emotional strength sustains it.
- Purpose aligns with it.
- Brotherhood strengthens it.
- Courage protects it.
- Fatherhood extends it.
- Service multiplies it.
- Legacy is built by it.
- Self-mastery keeps it alive.
- Resilience keeps it moving

This all stacks into one unshakable truth:— the Real Man is built daily, and hopefully what this book has shown you is that a Real Man doesn't wait for a mission to find him. He chooses it. Commits to it. And lives it—fully.

Because men on mission don't just change their lives, they change the world.

TAKE ACTION ON THESE THREE CHALLENGES.

1. Reflect: What in your life is worth fighting for, building for, or sacrificing for?
2. Write: Craft a personal mission statement. Short. Clear. Bold.
3. Act: Read it every day this week. Let it shape your decisions.

CONCLUSION

THE REAL MAN IS BUILT DAILY

This book may be ending—but your build has just begun. Being a Real Man doesn't happen overnight.

It isn't earned by titles or unlocked by age.

It's forged—daily, through deliberate decisions and quiet victories.

You won't always feel it. Some days, you'll fall short. You may wonder if it's even worth the work.

But those are the days that build you the most. You build when you speak truth even when your voice shakes. You build when you honor a commitment no one sees. You build when you walk away from what's easy and do what's right.

This isn't about perfection. It's about pursuit.

You lead yourself before you lead others. You learn to carry weight before your trusted with more. You build from the inside out—because that's where strength lasts.

This all starts with you every day.

Each morning, you get a choice. Build or drift. Rise or fold. Lead or blend in. The world is full of men who quit on themselves a long time ago. Don't join them. Build anyway. One small win a day. One stronger decision. One deeper commitment. Brick by brick. Trait by trait. **That's how Real Men are built.**

Final Words: Your Build, Your Legacy

The truth is simple: Your wife, your kids, your friends, your coworkers, they don't need a perfect man. They need a present man.

A man who owns his life and lives it with strength, humility, and intention, a man who thinks bigger; leads better, lives and loves stronger, and one who is building every day.

Take this book, these traits, and these challenges—and live them. Live them when no one's watching. Live them when it's inconvenient. Live them until they become who you are. Because you are being built every day.

The world is waiting for what you become.

THE REAL MAN CODE

A personal creed to revisit daily or pass down

These aren't just ideas. They're a way of life.

Sign your name to this code—not for perfection, but for pursuit.

THE CODE I LIVE BY:

1. I take full ownership of my choices, mistakes, and growth.
2. I protect those I love—physically, emotionally, spiritually.
3. I say what I mean and mean what I say.
4. I discipline myself so no one else has to.
5. I control my emotions instead of being controlled by them.
6. I serve before I lead, and I listen before I speak.
7. I walk with faith, lead with courage, and finish with honor.
8. I do not quit. I get back up. Every time.
9. I build men around me—I don't compete with them.
10. I think bigger—not for ego, but for impact.

Signed: _____

Date: _____

"The Real Man is built daily, and this is where he begins."

Declarations Page – "I Am That Man"

I am not perfect, but I am present.

I am not a coward. I show up.

I am not ruled by emotion. I lead it.

I do not run from responsibility. I carry it.

I don't hide in shame. I rise in strength.

I build myself so I can build others.

My character is my compass.

My faith is my foundation.

My purpose is my mission.

My legacy is being written—today.

I am a Real Man, and I will be built daily.

Signed: _____

Date: _____

Letter to the Next Generation

Dear Son, Brother, Nephew, Friend—

If you're reading this someday, know this:
The world will try to define you.
It will try to confuse you, distract you, numb you, or tempt you to shrink.

Don't fall for it.

A Real Man is not what the world makes of him.
A Real Man is what he builds—day after day, with love, grit, faith, and fire.

I've tried to live it. I've stumbled. I've risen.
And I hope this book helps you rise even faster.

You are more than your mistakes.
More than your fears.
You are built for purpose.

So build. Lead. Live.
The world is waiting for the man you choose to become.

— Someone who believes in you.

www.ingramcontent.com/pod-product-compliance
Lightning Source LLC
Chambersburg PA
CBHW031221120626
46545CB00003B/944